Self-Taught vs. Online Learning

Welcome to yet another step in your journey to break into the field of data. This is exciting because we're going to tackle one of the main questions people ask themselves when starting their journey to break into the field of data. It's good to ask this question as well- the people who don't end up doing as well in this field are the ones who get the idea they want to work in data, and immediately sign up for Udacity or some other online program. For them, when it gets tough, there's nothing motivating them to continue because they haven't thought about what they want exactly, and they haven't picked a method of learning that fits their goals.

This section is the perfect next step after you've read, "Choosing Your Path in Data", one of our other strategy sections. In, "Choosing Your Path" you'll have the tools to uncover exactly what path in data is right for you- some people are interested in pursuing Data Analyst and other analytics roles, while on the other end of the spectrum, some have the type of mind best suited to pursue Data Engineering roles. Whichever is the case for you, this section will be a fantastic resource to help you build the skills necessary to not only get those roles, but succeed in them. As we go through this material, we'll assume you've read the, "Choosing Your Path in Data" section and have a good idea of where you're heading.

The purpose of this section is to answer the age-old (sort of) question: Should I teach myself a certain set of skills, or should I take online classes? Because the data careers, and particularly Data Science, have become extremely popular only in the last few years, and online coursework hasn't been in the mainstream long either, no one has really tackled this question yet. Sure, you may find a few blog articles here and there, but there has been no long-form, detailed strategy section to really dig and and get the answer- until now.

This section will give you the framework to decipher whether you should focus mainly on looking for ways to teach yourself data skills (using books, online forums, articles, etc.), or if you should sign up for a full online course through a platform like Coursera. Once you understand your approach, you'll be able to move on to our other sections- for example, "Breakdown of Top 3 Online Learning Platforms" if you're going to online learning, or our "Essential Data Reading List". From there, you'll be able to dive in to the actual material.

Why This Chapter is Important

As you can tell by now, each section in our series is helping you build a strategy to ultimately get a fantastic job in the world of data, whether it's as a Data Analyst, Data Scientist, Data Engineer, or somewhere in between. This section is important because it's going to help you determine how you actually go about building the skills necessary. But why should we think about the "how"? Why not just save time and jump right in to a course or something, and then adjust later?

Many people feel that they should jump right into the material, and there's nothing wrong with poking around different data concepts to see what catches your eye. The problem is that you can spend a lot of time and a lot of money on something that isn't the best learning style for you, doesn't get you to your goals, is stressful rather than fun, and can leave you wondering why you're even doing it in the first place. A great strategy will set you on a path that is not only challenging, but interesting enough to get you through tough parts, and ultimately gets you to your goals. That is what we'll do in this section- let's dive in.

One of the most important things to think about initially is where you are and where you're going. "Where you are" essentially means your current level of skill working with data and how much you've worked with data in the past. There aren't hard and fast segments we can put you in, but here are a few potential groups:

Brand New

This category may fit you if you've never had a job where manipulating data was a part of your regular tasks. People in this category may have used data, whether it's in reporting, a spreadsheet, or something else, but have little to no experience analyzing or performing operations on the data. If you're not sure how to do formulas in Google Sheets or Excel, you're probably close to this category. Another good point of reference is your educational base- if your college major was something non-technical such as communications or English, it's another indicator that you might fall into this category (although recent experience is more relevant). If this is you, you may benefit from learning the basics in a well-structured online course.

Some Experience

Most job seekers looking to break into the field of data fall into this intermediate category, which describes those currently in a job that does some data work. This includes those in marketing roles who use Google Sheets or Excel to review lists and process results, and even certain sales roles have a small analytical element. This may also apply to you if you're working closely with Data Analysts or Data Scientists and have a birds-eye view of what their work looks like. This group has had a taste of the data world and wants more. If you can do basic formulas in spreadsheets, and consider yourself more analytically-minded, this is probably where you fit in. In terms of college experience you may or may not have had a more quantitative major, but regardless you likely gravitated toward technology and technical topics.

Already have a Role in Data

This is an interesting category because there are a lot of people who already have a role in data (typically as some sort of analyst) and want to move into something more advanced, or perhaps just do a similar role at a larger company that's difficult to get into. We see a lot of Marketing Analysts and Operations Analysts looking to become Data Scientists or Engineers at top tech company, and feel like they need help getting to the next step. If this is you, you'll know- generally if your day-to-day involves a lot of SQL querying and data manipulation, you have a data role. People in this bucket typically choose to teach themselves additional skills to move up to an advanced role, although it's not uncommon for them to take additional online coursework for topics that are very new to them.

These three buckets are a great guideline, but remember that this is a broad spectrum rather than a rigid classification. Where do you fit? Maybe you have some experience in data, but in terms of technical skills you pick things up quickly and are already moving on to move advanced topics such as SQL. Maybe you're doing a ton of data work and feel like you fit the "Already have a Role" bucket, but you don't have a technical title such as "Analyst" and your boss isn't technical either, so you feel like there are some gaps in your knowledge.

Next, we want to think about your outcome. If you've read our other sections, this is not new. Essentially we want to define what we're going after as our next move in the world of data, meaning the next role you're looking to enter. It doesn't have to be a long-term vision of where you want to be in five or ten years. All you need to do is define where you want to go next, and it starts with asking a few questions:

- What kind of work would I enjoy?

- What path in data is right for me (see our "Discover Your Path in Data" section)?

- What is a reasonable next step? Don't lower your sights, but also remember that there are certain roles that are very difficult to get and would require many years of work to even be considered.

- What type of company would I like to work at? Be flexible, but it's good to have some general guidelines.

Here's an example outcome: "My outcome is to have a fantastic role as a Data Analyst or Data Scientist where I tackle interesting problems at a top tech company"

One more: "My outcome is to break into the world of data by getting a great role within the Data Analyst path. I want to work at a company that is consumer-facing and mission-driven, and company size or prestige isn't as important to me."

What is your outcome? It doesn't have to be perfect, but go ahead and see what you can come up with. Make sure you write this down somewhere and don't just say it in your head- once you write things down they become more real, and many of the people who ultimately reach their outcome review it daily.

Last note on outcomes: they're flexible. You're not bound to anything when you write your outcome. We see many candidates who initially say they want to work at a startup, but after talking to lots of companies they decide they'd like to go for a more established company instead.

The opposite also happens frequently. You need to define your outcome in the early stages of your job search, but don't be afraid to change it up if you want to go a different direction.

As you're thinking about where you currently stand in your data knowledge and what you want to achieve, the next logical consideration is the distance between the two. How big is the gap between where you are and where you want to be? If you're currently a Data Analyst at a mid-sized tech company and want to be a Data Scientist at a larger company, the gap probably isn't too big. If you're currently working as a server at a restaurant and want to be a Machine Learning Engineer, that's probably a bigger gap. The general rule of thumb is that it will take more time and formal education (eg. actual classes) if you have a large gap, but there are certainly exceptions. Keep in mind that you will learn more about the distance as you apply for jobs- for example, "Data Scientist" can mean lots of different things, and companies often have a spectrum of levels for their Data Scientists- meaning it's potentially easier to get in at a lower level and work your way up.

This is also a good time to think about if aiming for a stepping-stone role is right for you. In the restaurant server example above, although he can definitely work his way into an ML Engineer role eventually, they'd probably have an easier time starting as an analyst or entry-level Data Scientist, and then building up the skills along the way.

One of the important things we're doing in all of our sections is coming to an understanding of who you are as it relates to your career and abilities in data. Reflect on this. The better you understand where you stand, the easier it will be to pick an effective strategy to get you to your goals. Choose your outcome, know yourself, define a strategy, execute, improve, repeat. That's all there is to it.

Factors to consider

Naturally there are some factors to consider when you're thinking about which educational direction is right for you. The important thing to note here is that while you should definitely give these things some thought, don't suffer from "Analysis Paralysis": when you're analyzing so many different things that you get overwhelmed and never end up taking any action at all. Our recommendation is to spend a few hours (or less) analyzing the below, write down your thoughts, and then move on. Let's jump in.

Cost

This is something on everyone's mind when they think about how they're going to pursue education in the data field- how much is it going to cost? There are two truths: the first is that it can cost a lot of money if you choose, and the second is that it doesn't have to cost anything (financially) if you choose. Your reality will likely be somewhere in the middle- you'll spend a little money on great content that helps you grow, but it won't be crazy amounts. Let's look at each option and figure out the investment required.

Self-Taught

Contrary to popular belief, "Self-Taught" doesn't mean "Free" for most people, although it's certainly possible to learn everything you need to know with just an internet connection and a browser. It depends on the individual's learning style, but most people get a lot of value from books and similar non-course content.

We'll take a look at some resources in the "Essential Reading" section, but good books relating to data concepts tend to cost somewhere between $15-45. You shouldn't need many, but a budget of a $100 would go a long way to building up your resources. One note- it's a good idea to start with one book and see how you like learning that way. Some people love reading from a physical book, while others simply don't learn well that way and prefer some kind of video content. Don't spend a bunch of money on books before you know you like to learn that way.

Online Courses

Most people expect that online courses will cost money, but there is a lot of mystery and guessing around exactly how much. Truthfully, it depends on which platform (eg. Coursera, Udacity) you choose, as well as which program or programs you do.

Additionally, what many people don't understand at first is that the majority of online learning platforms have free options that allow you to take full course content without paying anything at all. What it usually comes down to is if you want an official certificate or credential that shows you've completed the material, and if so you'll need to pay anywhere from a few hundred to a few thousand dollars.

If you end up deciding that online learning is a viable path for you, check out our popular strategy deep dive: "Breakdown of Top 3 Online Platforms". There we go into detail about the program structure of Udacity, edX, and Coursera, and we reveal crucial info to know such as the program types, costs, and credentials available. Make sure you head over to that section before signing up for anything.

Time

Another important factor to consider is how much time you want to spend learning before you're ready to look for a new job. This will play a big part in helping you determine which learning method to choose, because one path won't necessarily work for a given time constraint.

For example, if you have some good experience and want to start looking for new roles in a month, you probably won't want to sign up for a big online course. In that case you'd probably want to go the self-taught route and dig into the skills you need to build up.

On the other hand, if you're less constrained on time and are looking to be in a new role between six months to a year from now, you have more options. Even if you're already experienced in data, you may benefit from the structure and comprehensive coursework of a full online program, particularly if you're looking to enter a new field within data (eg. Data Engineering).

Credential

Whether or not you need a credential can vary on a lot of things, primarily what your education and work experience looks like. Many who work in a role that is far away from their goal, such as a server or some sort of blue-collar work feel that they need to get a degree or credential of some kind to make the leap to the corporate world, and that's often a good idea. In this case, online learning is probably the way to go since self-teaching obviously doesn't have any certification component.

Others have a good quantitative degree, and potentially even an advanced degree, and also have relevant work experience in data. For them, continuing education in order to pursue a new role is simply a matter of beefing up their skills so they can get qualified and do well in interviews. For these job-seekers, self-teaching is a more efficient way to reach their ultimate outcome.

Based on initial research for this strategy guide, most people fall somewhere in the middle. They are already in the corporate world, and have had some taste of data work, although they're not in a full data role yet. Their decision isn't as cut and dry as the above two examples, but many of them tend to lean more toward online coursework for the credentialing aspect because it gives them a great base of foundational knowledge, and the credential can't hurt.

For a more in-depth analysis on the topic of credentialing, take a look at our "Breakdown of Top 3 Online Learning Platforms" section. There we get into detail about the different types of credentials available and also dig into whether or not you actually need a verifiable certificate.

Current Position and Mobility

One of the important things many people forget to factor into their decision when looking to pursue a career in data is where they stand at their current employer and what the opportunities look like. One of the smartest things you can do, if at all possible, is to move into a data role within your current employer and learn on the job. We'll go ahead and lump this into the "self-taught" bucket, but in reality you'll be learning a lot from your environment and the people around you.

Here's an example: let's say you're a marketing coordinator at a small tech company and have been there for a year and a half. Assuming you're on good terms with your boss and the company itself, you can have a conversation about how you ultimately want to pursue data-driven roles, and would love to do it in your current company. If you see current job openings at your company, all the better. What many early-career people don't realize is that it's really expensive to hire from the outside, and there's a lot of uncertainty involved. Faced with the decision, most companies would rather move someone they know is reliable into a different role than let them leave the company and have to hire someone external for the role (not to mention backfilling the role the person left).

There is some nuance to this conversation, however. You can't just pull your boss aside and say you're going to quit if you can't move into an analyst role (for example). People don't like to be threatened, and it won't go well. What you can do is have an honest conversation about how you're passionate about working with data, are doing lots of work to learn things on your own, and ask their advice about how you could pursue something within the company. You want to be pleasant and don't make it seem like you're going to quit. Just let them know it's something you're working toward and would love the opportunity to do a role at your current company.

The pros of this approach are that you (should) already have a good reputation at your current company, which will make them more likely to want to move you. It's also likely that you won't be competing with as many people as you would on the open job market, or at least you'd have an advantage over them because you're a known quantity at your company.

The major con is that you'll almost certainly make less money than if you moved to the same role at a different company. Internal processes within companies can be quite rigid, and many won't do big pay increases, even if you enter a completely new role. That said, one great strategy is to move into a new, data-driven role at your current company if you can, and then later move to a different company after you've accumulated some experience and accomplishments for your resume. It's much easier to get a data role if you're already in a data role.

In summary, if you can move to a data role within your current company, you'll be able to learn a lot on the job and probably won't have to take a full online program. If this seems possible for you, go ahead and have that conversation with your boss and see what the options are. If it doesn't seem realistic because of your position (eg. you work at a restaurant), or your boss tells you it's not possible, an online program can be a great way to stick out in the job pool.

The Ideal Way to Learn

The last topic we'll go into has less to do with your background. Now we want to think about what your learning style is and how you'd do with the mediums we're discussing here. Think about your past- have you had success watching video courses online (for any subject), or have you done the best reading books and digging into things yourself? Remember that each way of learning has unique benefits: on the online learning side, for example, many people feel that the deadlines built into the program help them continue to move forward and push themselves to grow. On the other side, self-teaching allows you to take in a broad array of perspectives on topics and see other points of view- which can lead to a deeper understanding of the concepts.

Most people have some experience with both and can probably do OK with either learning style, but at the same time they tend to lean one way over the other. The easiest way for you to understand how online platforms or self-teaching work for you is to give them each a try. Remember that you don't have to fully commit to any learning program or any method at the beginning- you can and should "shop around" and see what suits you. We've got some great resources in our "Essential Data Reading List", and some of them are totally free and open-source. Definitely check those out. You can also look through our "Breakdown of Top 3 Online Learning Platforms" section and see what you can try out for free.

Once you get an idea of your learning style and what works best for you, you'll be able to add that to your evaluation process and choose the best path forward. Before you know it, you'll be on your way to an amazing and enjoyable career in data.

Final words

We're going to close this section out with a few final tips and words of advice. First of all, don't get overwhelmed by the choice between online learning and self-teaching. Even if you get it wrong and sign up for an online course that's not perfect for your needs, you can always remedy the situation by signing up for a different program or teaching yourself the skills you need.

On a similar note, know that it doesn't have to be one or the other. In this section we've been focused on getting you started on the right path so you can start making progress toward your goals as soon as possible. But this is just a starting place. Many people find themselves starting with one learning method, and then switching back and forth over time as they look for both wider and deeper knowledge in the field of data.

For example, one learner recently started by self-teaching basic concepts in Python and SQL, and applying them in his current job as much as possible. After some time, he realized that it would be hard to teach himself statistical concepts he needed to pursue a role in Data Science, so he took a full online program through Coursera. After a lot of work, this ultimately led to him getting a great role as a Data Scientist in a large, pre-IPO tech company. This is possible for you too.

Also keep in mind that whatever you skills and concepts you can apply in a business context will be most beneficial for your learning and for when you start interviewing. If at all possible, you want to apply what you're learning to your current role, even if it's extra stuff on top of your day job. Above we mentioned having a conversation with your manager about how you're looking to pursue a role in data, and you can also reach out to Data Analysts, Data Scientists, and Data Engineers within your company to learn about what they do and how you might apply it. When you use this approach, you don't have to narrowly focus on people in the same exact path you're ultimately pursuing (eg. Data Engineering). Feel free to meet and interact with anyone in the field of data- understanding all the different roles and how they work will benefit you greatly, because no one in any data roles works in a vacuum.

If you're not currently working, or it isn't possible to apply data skills to your current job, work on projects that have a business context or application. Most data education programs have a project component, where you put together a larger piece of work on your own (very common in programs that have a Machine Learning element). One mistake that many learners make is that they're not thoughtful about the type of project they do, and it ultimately doesn't resonate with the recruiter or hiring manager.

For example, there is a classic dataset with types of Irises (a flower), and a popular Machine Learning project is to build a model to predict the type of Iris given the features of a plant. This is great if you plan to go into horticulture, but it's unlikely to be impactful with a hiring team. What's the business application of the model? How does it apply to real-world problems?

As an exercise, let's take a look at three potential projects, all of which are possible via open-sourced datasets:

1. Predicting the type of Iris (Iris dataset)

2. Predicting neighborhoods in Brooklyn where crimes are most likely to occur in the future (Brooklyn Crime dataset)

3. Predicting user demand on Airbnb to determine the key markets for supply acquisition (Airbnb dataset)

Of these, which do you think would resonate most with a recruiter or hiring manager? We can safely exclude #1, as we already described. #2 is better, and probably more interesting- since police departments function as a business in many ways, you can add some "business" context into your project by talking about where you would invest resources to prevent future crimes. #3 is our best bet, since it is similar to real-world problems that a company would face. When you do this kind of project, you have the opportunity to create a plan describing the business problem, ideal outcome, and how you will get there using data.

Remember that hiring teams aren't going to have the time to look through all of your projects, and in all likelihood they're going to just skim one of them. Put your best and most interesting project first, and make sure it's one that applies to the business world. If you're not sure where to start, we recommend first compiling a list of datasets and APIs you can pull data from- go for well-known companies like Uber, Twitter, and Airbnb. Once you have your list of datasets and companies, do research on the problems and challenges these specific companies are facing. What is the biggest roadblock for Twitter right now? Is it fraud or abusive content? Does Uber trying to get more drivers or more passengers? Jot down a few bullet points about the challenges you're finding, and then link the source (usually a news article). When you create your project, you can even link to these articles to show that the problem you're solving is a real one. The last step before diving in is to check the datasets to make sure that the data available can be used to solve the problem. For example, if the Uber datasets or API doesn't have information on drivers, it would be hard to solve a problem on driver growth.

Once you have that figured out, go ahead and start your project. This isn't meant to be a guide on how to make a Data project for your portfolio, but hopefully this information points you in the right direction. Remember: when it comes to portfolios and projects, the more business relevance a project has, the better. Go for the ideas that are both interesting to you and can solve a real-world business problem (or at least a problem that could be real). This kind of project will have a bigger impact on the hiring team and increase your chances of success.

This is it. By now you've gotten an idea of the paths available to you and are probably starting to lean in the direction of either self-taught or online learning. Remember that it's important to think about this before your commit to something fully, but this isn't a forever decision- if you decide to self-teach for a few months and then move to an online program, you'll still be in great shape. In fact, most people see the choice between self-teaching and online learning not as "one or the other" but as a question of, "Where should I start?". Using that frame, the choice becomes easier. As a next step, go through this section and write down your thoughts. What are your decision points? Where do you fall into the buckets we described? What is available to you in your current role? As you review the information and write down your thoughts, the decision will become more clear. Additionally, if you'd like more detail on online programs, you can use the chapter: "Breakdown of the Top 3 Online Learning Platforms". There we have a breakdown of Udacity, edX, and Coursera, and go deep into the details about the coursework itself, costs associated, and credentialing opportunities.

www.ingramcontent.com/pod-product-compliance
Lightning Source LLC
Chambersburg PA
CBHW031510210526
45463CB00008B/3170